DEPERSONALIZATION DEREALIZATION DISORDER

THE SIX-WEEK JOURNEY TO MENTAL CLARITY

PANKAJ SHARMA

PANKAJ SHARMA

Depersonalization Derealization Disorder

The Six-Week Journey to Mental Clarity

First published by Amazon Kindle Direct Publishing (KDP) 2025

Copyright © 2025 by Pankaj Sharma

All rights reserved. No part of this publication may be reproduced, stored or transmitted in any form or by any means, electronic, mechanical, photocopying, recording, scanning, or otherwise without written permission from the publisher. It is illegal to copy this book, post it to a website, or distribute it by any other means without permission.

Pankaj Sharma asserts the moral right to be identified as the author of this work.

Please be advised that I am not a licensed mental health professional, psychologist, or psychiatrist. The content shared in this book is based solely on my personal experiences and reflections, and should not be construed as professional advice or guidance. If you or someone you know is in need of professional mental health support, I strongly encourage seeking the assistance of a qualified and licensed healthcare provider.

First edition

This book was professionally typeset on Reedsy. Find out more at reedsy.com

Contents

1	Introduction	1
2	What are Depersonalization and Derealization Disorders?	5
3	Challenges of Living with Depersonalization-Derealization	9
4	Lost in Myself: My Struggle with DPDR	13
5	The Foundation of Healing in DPDR	20
6	Common Mistakes in DPDR Recovery	28
7	Accurate Nutrition for Accelerated Recovery	34
8	Interdependence Among Dimensions of Well-Being	39
9	Harnessing Nature's Tools for Healing	44
10	Mindful Distraction: A Path to Temporary Solace	50
11	Six Weeks of Healing and Growth	53
12	Everyday Tools to Support Your Healing	71
13	Effective Ways to Manage DPDR Symptoms	74
14	The Power of Healing and Hope	80
	About the Author	84

1

Introduction

Depersonalization-Derealization Disorder(DDD)

Living in the 21st century is a blessing as technology has eased our lives to a greater degree—from lifestyle to education to healthcare to business. It has reduced the manual labor that used to demand a lot of time and effort from everybody for their daily tasks. However, it wouldn't be unfitting to say this is also an age of cut-throat competition in every possible field. The population is ever-growing, and so is the demand for food, land, healthcare, education, and all the essentials required for human beings to live peacefully.

As the population grows, the demand for all these essential resources grows, which causes people to wage literal war against each other for the best resources. Today's life is fast-paced, and there's no time to stop; otherwise, there will be a high chance of being left behind while others continue to move forth. Yes, this is a great time for everybody on this planet as there are ample opportunities for everyone because many unconventional doorways to earning a livelihood have opened up. However, these markets have been flooded due to competition.

In today's fast-paced world, maintaining optimal health is crucial for individuals to achieve their goals and experience a deep sense of fulfillment. Many people have unrealistic, one-dimensional ideas of health. Many consider a person healthy if they seem physically sound while others believe a person to be healthy if they check all the boxes of socially fitting behavior and conduct. However, holistic health is multi-dimensional. It's an absolute sync between an individual's faculties, be they physical, mental, or emotional. This fosters stability, harmony, and a profound sense of overall well-being within an individual.

Holistic health is achieved through the integration of physical, emotional, social, professional, spiritual, environmental, and intellectual well-being. A balance in all aspects of one's being is imperative to gaining holistic health. Due to the evolution of

INTRODUCTION

technology and the opening of gateways to unconventional opportunities, our lives and health should've improved manifold. Yet, as per the healthcare figures, people are spending a great fraction of their fortune on wellness more than ever. What's even more surprising to note is that, as per statistics, there's an upsurge in mental illnesses among the general population, and so is the treatment expenditure.

Also, there are a lot of stigmas in society regarding mental health issues, owing to a lack of knowledge and understanding of the human psyche. Many people are not able to wrap their heads around the possibility of a person being ill if physically they seem sound. The fact about a lot of mental illnesses like depression, anxiety disorders, schizophrenia, bipolar disorder, etc., is that a majority of symptoms run in parallel with each other, which makes it extremely challenging most times to diagnose the right disorder before the onset of treatment accurately.

While an absolute cure for mental illnesses may not be possible, significant improvements in quality of life can often be achieved over time. Psychiatrists prescribe different anti-anxiety and anti-depressive medicines to alleviate the symptoms. Psychologists arm patients with practical tools and behavioral techniques through Cognitive Behavioral Therapy (CBT) which helps improve their quality of life. However, unlike physical ailments, recovering from mental illness requires patients to take charge of their healing. Mental health professionals provide guidance and support, but true recovery depends on the patient's effort to rewire their mind and overcome their challenges.

The world is familiar with common mental health issues such as anxiety disorders, depression, mood disorders, obsessive-compulsive disorder (OCD), and various phobias. However, there are rare mental illnesses that even many mental health professionals are unaware of, affecting only a small percentage of the population. Due to the limited expertise available for treating such rare disorders, patients often face significant challenges in finding the help and support they need.

Depersonalization and Derealization Disorder is one such rare mental illness, affecting approximately 1–2% of the population. As there is no specialized treatment plan for this disorder, mental health professionals often rely on approaches developed for other mental illnesses with overlapping symptoms. However, the majority of those diagnosed see little substantial improvement in their quality of life.

So, what are depersonalization and derealization? Are they the same, different, or interlinked? Can someone be diagnosed with both simultaneously? What are the root causes of these disorders? We will explore these questions in detail in the next chapter.

2

What are Depersonalization and Derealization Disorders?

As per WebMD, Depersonalization disorder is associated with feelings of experiencing disconnection or detachment from one's body and thoughts whereas Derealization is a mental state where you feel detached from your surroundings. Reading these definitions may bewilder new readers who, until now, had no idea that such conditions could affect people, but unfortunately, they do. However, the disorder cannot be confined to a simple box of definitions, as these are just basic, generic ideas of what a person experiences. In reality, it is much more complex. Depersonalization and/or Derealization Disorder is an eerie state of existence due to an altered brain chemistry stimulated by different factors. These are dissociative disorders that cause detachment, leading to a feeling of alienation from one's self and surroundings. Depersonalization in layman's terms refers to feeling detached from one's natural state of existence in life while Derealization refers to detachment from the natural environment or surroundings. When the detachment is transient, one returns to one's original state of existence. However, if the detachment is long-lasting, the individual transitions into a new state of existence due to rewired brain chemistry.

Both Depersonalization(DP) and Derealization(DR) can have an array of root causes that are diverse and unrelated to each other. Below are the observed root causes, as shared by different people on various forums, that they believed triggered the symptoms and caused early signs of DPDR:

1. *Use of recreational drugs such as Marijuana (weed)*
2. *Certain medications prescribed to treat existing physical or mental ailments*
3. *The aftermath of a traumatic event or PTSD*
4. *Neurological disorders*
5. *Childhood trauma*
6. *Pre-existing mental illnesses like prolonged stress, depression, anxiety, or mood disorder*
7. *Hyperawareness of the self and surroundings*

The aforementioned are just a few of the causes; however, they vary from person to person. The onset of DP-DR symptoms can be triggered by different factors, and there is no established set of events behind it. Whether these feelings are transient or remain persistent depends on how critically they affect the individual and how they deal with them. Some people recover within a few days, while others may take weeks, months, or even years to heal. However, for many, recovery is not fully achieved, and they continue to live with the disorder for years or even decades. They learn to manage their symptoms and alleviate psychological and psychosomatic pain often with the help of mental health professionals, who provide medications, therapies, and practical coping tools and techniques to navigate and manage challenging situations. Nonetheless, the quality of life for such patients often plunges to its lowest point. The neuroplasticity in their brains reshapes their neural pathways in such a way that living with DP-DR becomes an existential reality, making it immensely challenging for them to revert to their earlier state of ideal existence before slipping into the DP-DR coma.

Below are the symptoms commonly experienced by DP-DR patients:

1. *The immediate surroundings feel unnaturally large and threatening.*
2. *Vision may appear blurred, dull, or gray, accompanied by sensations of losing vision or going blind; floaters are often noticed in the air.*
3. *Body parts, such as arms, legs, or fingers, feel unreal, as though they don't belong to the person. Reflections in the mirror appear distorted, making it seem like one is looking at a different person.*
4. *A constant sense of observing one's actions from an external perspective, as though being an outsider to oneself.*
5. *Emotional numbness, with an inability to connect to family, friends, or relationships.*
6. *An overwhelming fear of losing sanity or developing severe mental health conditions like dementia or psychosis.*
7. *Development of specific phobias, such as agoraphobia.*

DP-DR can also be triggered by pre-existing mental health conditions such as anxiety disorders, depression, and mood disorders, or physical ailments like vestibular issues, including dizziness, balance problems, vertigo, etc, leading to nausea, and vomiting. The symptoms experienced by patients can vary widely depending on individual factors. As previously discussed, the primary challenge in addressing mental illnesses lies in the overlapping of major symptoms, which often complicates accurate diagnosis and the development of an effective treatment plan.

Why do some people feel stuck in the loop of Depersonalization-Derealization, while others seem to recover in just days or weeks? What makes it so hard for some to heal, even after years or decades? And why doesn't therapy or psychiatric help always lead to the recovery we hope for in DP-DR cases? We'll dive into these questions in the next chapter!

3

Challenges of Living with Depersonalization-Derealization

Normally, when someone gets injured, they need immediate medical attention. The aftermath involves a lot—procedures, medications, follow-up visits, bills—and, of course, time, energy, and pain. Yet, once a specialist tends to the injury, we begin to feel a sense of safety. Even if the pain is intense (sometimes excruciating), we don't obsess over it. At first, we may focus on the pain, but eventually, we stop thinking about it constantly because we trust that it will heal over time. We rely on the safety net created by the doctor, believing in their expertise. As we get better, our attention shifts back to the normal parts of our lives—work, family, friends, and so on—until the injury is mostly forgotten. While we stay cautious and learn from the experience to protect ourselves in the future, we no longer dwell on it.

However, when it comes to mental illnesses like anxiety, depression, or depersonalization and derealization disorder, we become obsessed with the onset of symptoms 24/7 because we're dealing with ourselves—our psyche, to be specific. There's no pre-constructed safety zone or net from mental health professionals; they can only guide us in the right direction, but the work of healing ultimately lies on our shoulders. As humans, we constantly doubt ourselves, especially when it comes to our minds and thoughts. We tend to believe negative thoughts more than positive ones because of the protective nature of our brain, which is wired to identify threats both inside and outside our physical boundaries. The frightening thoughts feel overwhelmingly real, and the symptoms magnify the experience. Once the obsession with the symptoms begins, their grip on our subconscious becomes strong, making it incredibly difficult to find a coping mechanism that can counter these troubling thoughts and lay the foundation for healing. This is where we get stuck—a loop of repeating thought patterns and behaviors, which wires the brain to solidify the current beliefs and perceptions about this new existential reality. As time goes on, a person's reality aligns with this new mental frequency. As the cycle continues for months, years, or even longer, the subconscious mind becomes reprogrammed, and the distorted reality of depersonalization and derealization disorder feels like the world as it should be perceived by the sensory receptors.

There is no dedicated treatment course for DP-DR in the mental health community, unlike other more common disorders such as anxiety and depression. Even many mental health professionals, such as psychiatrists, clinical psychologists, and therapists, are not aware of this disorder or do not have the expertise to treat it. Most professionals approach treatment based on the symptoms, which overlap with other disorders. They often prescribe medications to manage anxiety and depression, which are also symptoms of DP-DR, in an attempt to alleviate the psychological pain caused by the symptoms. Additionally, many turn to Cognitive Behavioral Therapy (CBT), which involves talk therapy and behavioral techniques to help patients manage their symptoms, improve their quality of life, and progress in healing. However, this may not lead to complete recovery unless a sense of safety begins to develop over time, allowing the person to gradually achieve a state of wellness.

Depersonalization and Derealization are not life-threatening, but they make patients feel as though they are. The symptoms keep individuals constantly on guard, in a heightened state of awareness of both their surroundings and themselves, which they perceive as a threat—rather than seeing it as a natural phenomenon of the universe, as someone without DP-DR might experience it.

The biggest challenge of all is helping others understand how one feels when dealing with DP-DR. It's nearly impossible to articulate these feelings in a way that's easily relatable, which makes it hard for others to truly understand. Most of the time, individuals who are suffering from these feelings struggle to grasp them themselves and often find it exhausting to make others understand what they're going through.

In the beginning, many people with DP-DR are in a constant fight-or-flight state due to the adrenaline rush that keeps them alert to potential threats in their immediate surroundings or within themselves. This relentless state of alertness can drain them to the point of complete shutdown—mentally, emotionally, physically, socially, and environmentally. Later, when they start to understand the reasoning behind their terrifying symptoms through online resources such as help forums, support groups, and medical articles, they may feel a slight sense of relief, knowing others have been experiencing the same distressing symptoms for a long time.

However, this doesn't bring them any closer to recovery. Spending too much time, energy, focus, and attention in these support groups or forums often keeps people stuck in an obsessive-compulsive loop of symptoms.

Not being able to make loved ones, such as family or friends, understand their state during a time when they need every bit of support only deepens the patient's sense of isolation. Since everything appears physically normal, family and friends often find it difficult to relate to or understand their situation, despite their desire to help in any way they can. This challenge isn't limited to loved ones—many mental health professionals also struggle to comprehend the symptoms as described by patients. As a result, they tend to take a broad treatment approach, similar to how they would treat other mental illnesses with overlapping symptoms. Unfortunately, this approach only adds to the frustration, as it leaves patients feeling more misunderstood and neglected. Instead of receiving the specific care needed, they often feel stuck in a cycle of treatment that doesn't truly address the core of their struggles. It's not just the isolation from loved ones, but the lack of a personalized approach from professionals that prolongs the pain and hinders recovery.

4

Lost in Myself: My Struggle with DPDR

It was the end of 2017/beginning of 2018 when the circumstances had become quite stressful for me as I was juggling a lot of things at once. At the beginning of 2017, my uncle passed away, which had a profound effect on my family. The loss created a heavy atmosphere at home, and for a long time, everything felt weighed down by it. I didn't fully grasp how deeply it was affecting me back then, but over time, I could feel its emotional toll, even if I couldn't recognize it for what it was at the time.

By the end of 2017, I was in my last year of Engineering, and the placement season was at its peak. It felt like everything depended on what happened next. There was a lot of pressure to succeed, but I was mentally and emotionally exhausted by the events that unfolded in the last few months. The rigorous procedure which involved preparing, applying, testing, and interviewing was draining, and every rejection just undermined my confidence even more. Every "no" added more weight to what I was already carrying, leaving me worried about what lay ahead. My mind was constantly racing, caught up in a whirlwind of worry and panic, which made me wonder if things would ever get better.

On top of all that, I was tutoring a group of students in my area. What started as a way to keep myself busy and make some extra money soon became a huge responsibility. It wasn't just about teaching; it was about helping these kids grow, encouraging them, and giving them everything I had to help them succeed. But with everything else going on, it felt like I was juggling too many things at once. The emotional stress, mixed with additional responsibilities, made it feel like anxiety seemed to seep into all areas of my life.

Then, just when I thought things couldn't get any worse, I hit another wall. After making it to the final round of interviews for a job I was really positive about, I suddenly found myself passing out one morning after a simple trip to the store. It wasn't just a typical fainting spell; it felt like my body completely shut down. The experience was terrifying. My family rushed me to the hospital, where they discovered I had pneumonia. But the doctors didn't realize that I had been dealing with a long-running illness, misdiagnosed and treated with the wrong medications. All of this had thrown my body off balance, leading to the collapse. What I thought was just a small fever turned out to be much worse.

Everything—the family struggles, the pressure of college placements, the part-time tutoring job, and the health scare—started to feel like too much to handle. But somehow, I kept pushing through, hoping things would eventually calm down. Every day felt like a struggle, but the hope that things would get better is what kept me going, even when I wasn't sure how I would make it through.

Things started to shift after I was discharged from the hospital. Coming back home, I was no longer the same person. While there was good news waiting for me—getting selected by the last company I interviewed with—it didn't bring me the joy I had expected. The petrifying experience of collapsing at home and then returning after being discharged had changed me. My world felt different. I became hyper-aware of everything happening inside my body—how my organs were functioning, how the blood was circulating through my veins, how much pressure the veins exerted against my muscles, and how my breath moved through my lungs. I was fixated on these details as if I were a microscopic being scanning every part of myself from head to toe. This wasn't just a passing phase. Hours turned into days, and days into months, but the obsession remained constant. I was completely disconnected from the world outside my body.

The real trauma, however, was just beginning. As time went on, I started constantly searching for symptoms within myself. This became my full-time job for the next few months—investing myself entirely in my physical existence and searching for signs of a terminal illness. My anxiety only grew, reaching levels that could only be described as psychosomatic. Soon, I was consumed by the fear of having a serious illness that could wipe me out. I developed a terrifying, irrational fear of dying, particularly from the imagined pain that would come with it.

I experienced a range of symptoms—muscle tension, dizziness, balance issues, tinnitus, headaches, blurred vision, nausea, and many others. The list was endless. At times, I convinced myself I had a brain tumor or was having a stroke, leading me to undergo MRI scans. At other times, I feared I had a heart condition that could end my life at any moment, prompting me to get an ECG. I became convinced I had Parkinson's, epilepsy, multiple sclerosis—and every possible terminal illness. I dragged my parents to the hospital constantly, insisting on tests for every new disease I thought I had. Despite all the tests coming back clear, my fears didn't subside. The doctors assured me I was physically healthy, but my thoughts continued to spiral.

Eventually, things took a turn for the worse. I started feeling like a stranger to myself. As I tried to reconnect with the outside world, everything felt distorted. Normal objects—buildings, trees, people—looked strange to me, as if I were in a dream. It was as though I was awake but trapped in a drowsy state, unable to make sense of anything. I began experiencing constant panic attacks, overwhelmed by the very idea of existence. I couldn't recognize myself in the mirror, and my own body felt foreign—like someone else's hands and feet. It was the most terrifying experience, like being trapped in a horror movie with no escape.

Soon, I became numb. I couldn't cry, laugh, or feel any emotion. I couldn't connect with my family or friends. It felt like my body was shutting down to protect me, just like a computer shuts down to avoid overloading. But in my case, the constant mental strain kept my brain from shutting down naturally, leading to insomnia. Over time, my body's only way to cope was to disconnect from emotions, memories, and feelings—essentially shutting down the system. This only made me more terrified, as my perception of reality became increasingly distorted. The more I struggled, the more it fed my anxiety, depression, and fear of losing my sanity.

I sought help from both a psychiatrist and a psychologist, but my search for answers was in vain. Unfortunately, many mental health professionals don't fully understand this rare disorder. They often treat the symptoms with medications and therapies designed for more common issues like anxiety and depression, which provide temporary relief but not long-term solutions. Despite all the tests and treatments, I still couldn't find anyone who could explain or help me with what I was going through.

After some time, I started feeling more depressed, and the suicidal thoughts became more frequent. I just wanted to feel alive again and break free from the dissociative state I was stuck in. I yearned for the psychological pain to end and to reach a place of emotional release. But no matter what I tried, nothing seemed to help with my healing. I sought support in every way I could – joining DP-DR forums, Facebook groups, and YouTube channels – trying to understand the disorder and its root cause. However, the more I read, the more my attention and focus went into the problem itself. The deeper I dug, the more trapped I felt in my thoughts.

As time passed, I lost hope for recovery. The pain became unbearable as I questioned myself endlessly: "Why did this happen to me? What did I do to deserve this? Why did I focus so much on my internal world even when all my tests came back normal? Why did I fall into this cycle of thoughts that led to dissociation and, eventually, DP-DR?" I spent months stuck in this phase, lost and overwhelmed.

Eventually, I reached a breaking point. The weight of everything was too much, and I decided I couldn't keep living in this torment. During this time, I could not continue with my first job, lost connection with my family, and friends, and most importantly, disconnected from myself. Even though I knew everything around me was real, my perception of it felt like a stab of a knife, constantly reminding me of the distorted world I was living in. Yet, there was still a small part of me that refused to let go of hope. This tiny part of me clung to the memories of a time when everything felt normal, when I felt truly connected to life and the world around me.

One day, I reached an emotional breaking point. I was completely exhausted from the life I had subconsciously created for myself. It was time for me to let go of the past and make room for new growth. I became tired of asking "why" and "how" this all happened. Slowly, I began entering a new phase of acceptance. I started to come to terms with my reality. I decided to accept my condition, not with my heart fully healed, but with the determination to move forward despite everything I was feeling. It wasn't an easy choice, but I realized I had no other option but to move forward.

I decided to treat myself and heal, even when I didn't know exactly how that would happen. When all options seem impossible, the only thing left to rely on is faith in your own ability to heal. I refused to accept that complete recovery wasn't possible. I promised myself I would never give up, and I would explore every avenue, discovered or undiscovered, to heal. Despite the uncertainty, I knew I couldn't stay in this cycle forever.

So, I accepted my condition and made the conscious choice to move forward in my life. Even though I still had to endure the feelings that came with DP-DR, I knew that this decision was my only way out. I decided to take one step at a time, no matter how small, and not let myself get stuck in this loop again.

5

The Foundation of Healing in DPDR

Depersonalization and Derealization Disorders are assumed to be the brain's natural mechanism to protect itself from further deterioration while it undergoes an overload in the form of flooding emotions and obsessive-intrusive thoughts, whose by-products are stress, anxiety, and depression. To protect the brain from further impairment, the brain's limbic system, which is responsible for emotional and behavioral responses, is dynamically forced to shut itself down. Because a person with DPDR perceives both themselves and their immediate surroundings as constant threats, this triggers an "amygdala hijack," activating the sympathetic nervous system in response, which controls the body's involuntary responses. The body's "fight or flight response" gets activated, causing a variety of symptoms such as rapid heartbeat, quickened breathing, dilated pupils, etc. An individual could experience frequent panic attacks triggered by seemingly anything and everything and also develop different phobias, such as agoraphobia.

As I mentioned earlier, these symptoms can be managed with

medications like Selective Serotonin Reuptake Inhibitors (SSRIs), which are some of the most commonly prescribed antidepressants because they're generally safe and have only a few side effects. Therapies can also help you regain control of your mind. However, while these solutions can provide temporary relief by easing the symptoms for a while, true and permanent recovery requires a complete transformation in every area of life. And the truth is, no one can make that happen except you.

There's no magical pill or procedure that could make this disorder disappear from your life overnight. This fact must be repeated to oneself all the time, as people with DPDR become hopeless due to prolonged suffering and start looking for solutions that promise magical recovery. It's not possible! Complete recovery is probable, but not overnight, and living in a delusion of accidentally encountering a magical recovery aid won't help you recover at all; it's only going to push you away even further.

Acceptance is the foundation of permanent recovery. It is the key to the door that opens several pathways to self-healing, and yet it is extremely difficult to accept the undesirable aspects of life, whatever they may be. When anything unpleasant happens to us—be it in our career, relationships, physiologically, or emotionally—it directly impacts our mental health. A majority of people find it difficult to accept the unpleasant things that happen to them, leading to resentment in varying degrees across individuals. People find temporary solace in resentment for a long time, sometimes forever. It becomes incredibly challenging for them to move on in life—the cycle of painful thoughts never stops: "Why did it happen to me?", "What wrong did I do to deserve this?", "Why is life unfair to me?", etc. The continuous loop of negative emotions such as resentment, hatred, guilt, self-pity, and fear blocks the person from moving forward in life.

However, when a person reaches the stage of acceptance in life—of things, situations, circumstances, and their current reality—it allows them to break free of this infinite, continuous loop of negative emotions. This propels them to focus on the future and move on with life. What has happened has happened and isn't going to change; the past cannot be altered, and the painful memories are never going to vanish from our minds until our existence ceases. But once we accept our past for whatever it was, no matter how unfortunate and painful it may have been, it loses its power to affect our present. These memories no longer hinder our growth in life. While they are crucial, serving as a guiding force to carefully make future decisions, they must not hold us back in the past, preventing us from living in the present or losing our independence to create a beautiful, secure future.

Depersonalization-Derealization Disorder is a harsh reality for many people around the world. For countless individuals, it's a daily torment that has lasted for years. There's an emptiness in life, and a person becomes numb to most aspects of their existence—whether physical, mental, emotional, spiritual, social, or occupational. The experience is beyond words, and it's even more difficult to help others understand what one is going through, to make them relate, or to explain the struggle in search of treatment or a solution. The biggest challenge, however, is accepting the disorder itself. This is where many people get stuck, unable to break free from the obsessive-compulsive cycle of living with DPDR.

THE FOUNDATION OF HEALING IN DPDR

DPDR is not merely intrusive thoughts—it's a profound transformation of one's being and life, a complete shift in reality and perception. Yet, despite its intensity, it is entirely harmless. It doesn't threaten one's life; a person can continue living just as anyone else would. Still, these thoughts can cause pain that's as great as, or even greater than, any physical injury. In the case of physical injuries, the pain subsides with time, healing occurs, and it becomes a distant memory that no longer affects the present or future, as there is no fear involved. But in the case of a mental ailment like DPDR, the pain remains, sustained by the fuel of ongoing fear and uncertainty, and it continues to exist until we learn how to stop feeding it.

Fear is the fuel that keeps DPDR alive and maintains its hold on a person's psyche. It is the primary force that prevents one from reaching the stage of 'acceptance' with DPDR. As we've discussed before, DPDR deceives the mind into believing that one's immediate surroundings and even oneself are threats— dangers that could cause harm. This illusion keeps fear very much alive. For recovery to begin, fear must be confronted and overpowered.

But how does one overcome fear? It's easier said than done. It's not a simple task, and it's far more complex than it may seem. I know these are the thoughts that will probably arise when a statement like that is made—and they're true. It's not easy, especially when striving for lasting recovery. It requires tremendous effort, perseverance, sincerity, and consistent action, even in the face of setbacks. It demands unwavering hope and the belief that recovery is possible. Ultimately, it's about rewiring your brain to adopt an attitude that accepts nothing less than full recovery. Only when you truly believe in this will you be motivated to pursue it—and, most importantly, to work for it—regardless of whether results come quickly or take time.

So, the big question remains: How does one move past their fear to embrace and accept DPDR?

First of all, it's really important to understand how this fear stems in the case of DPDR. What keeps this fear alive, which in turn causes DPDR to persist? How does fear entangle a person in an infinite loop of intrusive thought patterns? How does fear obstruct the doorway leading to recovery? So, here it goes!

In the case of DPDR, the sensory perception of an individual shifts due to dissociation, and how the brain processes information about the surroundings and the self changes drastically due to rewired brain connections formed over time and altered brain chemistry brought about by external or internal stimuli. Perceiving the immediate surroundings and one's self as threats, owing to the feeling of unreality, gives birth to fear, which is a natural human tendency to develop. This fear continues to magnify over time when these feelings/emotions prolong, leading to an ever-looping cycle of intrusive OCD thoughts. As already discussed before, fear leads to an intrusive thought pattern, which results in the birth of all the undesirable physical manifestations of these thoughts in the form of undesirable psychosomatic symptoms.

When the fear of one's thoughts and symptoms grows manifold with time, it is followed by amygdala hijack or the fight-or-flight response, panic attacks, tormenting anxieties, and escalating depression over time. This gives a clear picture of how one's response to a situation, circumstances, present reality, and other things in life can lead to a profound shift in their perception of self, reality, and overall well-being. The key to coming out of this seemingly ever-going loop is addressing the cycle at its root, i.e., being mindful of how you respond to your sensory perception in the case of Depersonalization and Derealization.

Until now, you've been addressing the feelings of unreality with fear, which continued to fuel it and prolonged its longevity. However, you can break this habit over time by responding to these inescapable feelings, thoughts, and symptoms with a different approach. Instead of reacting in a petrifying manner, you should combat these with a mindful approach. Mindfulness is not anything new that people are not aware of, but how it must be practiced is mastered only by a small population in the world. Mindfulness is having complete awareness of oneself and the surroundings without reacting to the stimulus and trying not to perceive information through the judgment lens.

In the case of DPDR, you can only be enabled toward mindfulness if you have a thorough understanding of why you have been experiencing feelings of unreality and what the root cause of Depersonalization and Derealization is. DPDR is nothing abnormal; it's a natural, normal human brain mechanism to protect and preserve itself from further damage caused by the prolonged severity of load in the form of stress, anxiety, depression, etc., resulting from dissociation from the surroundings and the self. Due to this, the brain is forced to shut down its emotional responses and protect itself from further degradation.

Once you've achieved a state of clarity within yourself about DPDR, it will be easier to switch to your mindful gear to commence the transformation. So, if you experience DPDR next time, follow the method shared below to address the feelings and symptoms:

Mindful Method to Master the Fear of Unreality:

1. *As you observe your immediate surroundings or yourself, don't try to combat the undesirable, intrusive thoughts that arise, along with the inescapable feelings and symptoms they bring. Instead of fully believing your thoughts, observe them, letting them pass through your mind without judgment.*
2. *Question these intrusive thoughts whenever fear begins to take hold, as fear takes over the moment you start believing these thoughts as existential reality. Repeatedly questioning and countering these thoughts over time will help you stop believing them, which, in turn, will reduce your fear.*
3. *When you experience DPDR, don't react with fear or any negative emotion—just allow it to be. Then, redirect your full attention to something else, such as an object in your room, a word on a page, a character in a movie, or even a thought unrelated to DPDR.*
4. *These thoughts, feelings, and symptoms will seem more real than anything else only if you believe them immediately without a second thought. Observing them from a distance, questioning them, and not perceiving them through a judgmental lens will train your brain over time to stop reacting with fear or negative emotions—even when these thoughts feel threatening and symptoms seem to torment you.*

Your current state of existence is a result of your past behavioral patterns, and the behavioral patterns you begin to form in the present will gradually transform your brain chemistry and life moving forward.

6

Common Mistakes in DPDR Recovery

Out of the rare 1-2% of the population suffering from DPDR, only a few manage to recover completely. Some recover by 50-70%, while others learn to manage their symptoms over time. However, a large portion of the population continues to struggle under its weight. The people who recover from DPDR don't rely on a magical pill or undergo a life-altering procedure that heals them overnight. Recovery demands time, patience, persistence, and unwavering hope—without any guarantees or promises of success.

The recovery timeline varies from person to person—some recover in weeks or months, while others take years. It always begins with gaining a thorough understanding of their condition and continues with exploring all available alternatives to recovery. Once a person is fully equipped with the knowledge and understanding of what needs to be done, the actual recovery phase begins.

People who recover completely are typically solution-oriented.

They don't allow themselves to get tangled in the cobweb of theories, experiments, delusions, or futile discussions. They accept their condition and move forward in life, even when their perception makes everything feel fake, and their existence seems like a lie. Despite this, they don't lose their grip on the thread that connects them to their reality—the one they've known and grown up with.

Then there are those who remain trapped in intense remorse over their actions that led them to their current state of existence. They constantly whimper about having the disorder, desperately trying to escape their reality by employing all kinds of mental tricks to convince themselves they no longer have DPDR—only to be painfully proven wrong every time. This is one of the biggest mistakes people with DPDR make, as it keeps them from becoming ready for recovery. Yes, *ready* for recovery. It may sound strange to talk about "becoming eligible" for recovery, but it's not strange at all. Recovery always begins with acceptance. Unless we reach a point where we are no longer held back by negative emotions like guilt and fear, and instead feel propelled to explore healing possibilities, we aren't truly moving toward recovery.

Another significant mistake many people make is failing to step away from support groups, discussion forums, and DPDR communities. While these groups can be immensely helpful initially—offering an understanding of the disorder, a sense of belonging, and relatability with others who are on the same journey—they often become a crutch. People get excessively attached, engaging 24/7 in conversations about symptoms, recovery stories, hopelessness, and countless tips and techniques. These discussions frequently involve suggestions of medications like antidepressants and anti-anxiety drugs, or various other methods, shared by individuals who may or may not be qualified to provide such advice.

Even medical professionals don't have a universally effective or certified treatment for DPDR. That's not to say these communities don't serve a purpose, but prolonged involvement can have unintended negative consequences. The foundation of recovery from DPDR is reconnecting with reality, yet spending too much time in these groups often pulls people away from that goal.

Recovery requires stepping out of the dreamlike state DPDR creates and reestablishing a connection with reality. To achieve this, it's essential to focus on real-life activities and relationships, away from the constant cycle of online discussions and advice-seeking. Initially, these activities may feel shallow or insincere, but over time, they plant subconscious seeds of connection. Gradually, you begin to truly reconnect—with people, your surroundings, and, most importantly, yourself.

Let's read about how a 20-year-old girl named Stephanie reversed her condition and began enjoying life again:

Stephanie is experiencing Dissociation while grief-stricken

Stephanie, a 20-year-old first-year student at the University of Michigan, has always been a smart, cheerful, and positive girl. However, the life-altering event of losing her mother sent her into a deep state of shock and despair. She withdrew from her friends, relatives, and people in general, locking herself in her room all day for months. Even her interactions with her dad and siblings reduced significantly. As she was the closest to her mother, the loss hit her the hardest. She spent her days grieving and being consumed by endless looping thoughts about life and death.

One day, it was as if she woke up from a deep sleep, only to find herself in an alternate reality where everything seemed surreal—frighteningly so. It felt like she was living in a dream.

She couldn't connect with her reflection in the mirror, as though she was staring at a stranger. Terrified and unable to find a rationale for her bizarre experience, she started believing irrational things—like being possessed or even dead.

After intensely researching her symptoms on the internet, she discovered information about Depersonalization and Derealization Disorder (DPDR) and realized she wasn't alone. Stephanie had already mourned and suffered enough by this point and decided she wanted to live again. She made the courageous choice to accept both her past and her current state, enabling her to move forward.

Stephanie decided to reconnect with her old self by doing the things she once loved. Even though these activities felt fake or deeply unpleasant due to her symptoms, she pushed herself to do them anyway. Slowly but steadily, she began inching closer to her true self, reconnecting with reality, and rediscovering the joy of living. When you think about it, recovering from DPDR is a simple process, but the challenge lies in convincing the depersonalized human psyche to believe it.

Sample Exercise:

1. Pick an activity you've always enjoyed—something you may no longer do or feel capable of enjoying. For example, listening to your favorite music.
2. Choose an engaging movie or series and start watching it. Even if you feel consumed by your symptoms and unpleasant feelings while doing so, try to focus entirely on the experience.

3. As you watch, intrusive thoughts and feelings will arise. The characters, plot, surroundings, sounds, and dialogues may feel shallow, fake, or distant. Your mind will likely drift toward your symptoms and discomfort. But here's the key: **push yourself into the experience.** Use all your energy to focus fully on the movie or series, immersing yourself as much as you can. Initially, your attention might be only 5–10%, but as you repeat this exercise, your involvement will grow. Over time, you'll find yourself engaging more—reaching 50–60% attention, or even more. During this process, you're retraining your brain, rewiring your mind to focus on the experience instead of DPDR-related thoughts. Gradually, the activity will begin to feel real and enjoyable again.
4. Through consistent effort, you'll notice a transformation. Your symptoms will no longer dominate your experience, and you'll rediscover pleasure in the little things, like watching a movie. It's important to remember that this transformation may take days or even weeks, depending on the sincerity and consistency of your efforts.

7

Accurate Nutrition for Accelerated Recovery

Food fuels both physical and mental well-being

Food and water are the basic survival needs of any living being without which life cannot be imagined. The nutrition from food nourishes our body and mind by acting as the fuel needed to run the human life vehicle. Water, as we all know, makes up approximately 60% of the human body composition. It is the basis of existence on this planet. Despite the diverse food choices among different nations, communities, and tribes—shaped by factors like agriculture, culture, and traditions—no two individuals' food preferences are exactly alike. It's no secret that the food and diet choices we make shape our bodies and minds, much like our actions shape our lives. The correlation coefficient between diet and the human psyche is generally positive. Food plays a prominent role in shaping a person's psyche. A person's health directly affects how they feel and behave because food not only provides nutrition but also influences the production of various hormones through chemical reactions in the body. A person's state of mind and mood at any given time largely depend on the meals they've previously had E.g., beverages like Tea and Coffee contain a chemical called caffeine, which acts as a stimulating agent. It provides a quick boost of energy, making a person more alert and awake, but it can also lead to anxiousness or restlessness in some individuals. Similarly, confections-food items rich in sugar and carbohydrates—can have a drug-like effect on the brain by stimulating the release of endorphins, which help manage pain and stress. While each meal provides transient effects, consistent eating habits have the potential to subtly shape a person's psyche over time. For example, a cup of coffee might offer a quick energy boost but can lead to restlessness and increased anxiety shortly afterward. Prolonged caffeine consumption may cause persistent anxiety and increase vulnerability to mental health issues such as anxiety disorder.

As discussed earlier, the physical and mental dimensions of a human being are interrelated and have a strongly positive dependency on each other. All the dimensions of human existence-mental, emotional, social, spiritual, etc., are interdependent on one another. This is a fact backed by science! Anxiety or nervousness can cause an upset stomach, a rapid increase in heartbeat, sweating, and other symptoms. Similarly, a depressed person becomes sluggish and provides an abode for a host of physical ailments as a person's psyche functions like the CPU of the human body's hardware. As the brain's processing capacity reduces, the body's reflexes may lag, leading to various malfunctions within the body which is similar to how computer applications become unresponsive due to insufficient free available memory for the CPU to process them faster.

As established above, food is one of the pivotal factors in healing- be it mental or physical. The question is: Are we leveraging it to our maximum benefit? If food habits are developed strategically and food choices are made consciously, they can have miraculous long-term effects on an individual's mental health, specifically benefiting those with depersonalization-derealization disorder (DPDR). As with other physical or mental ailments, adjusting food habits can significantly propel the recovery process for DPDR patients.

Recovering from DPDR requires more than just patience; it also demands a thoughtful balance between eating healthy and allowing yourself small indulgences. Treating yourself to foods you love can boost your mental well-being, especially during those challenging moments when things feel overwhelming.

Steps to Accelerate Healing:

1. **Prioritize a Balanced Diet:** Focus on consuming a diet

rich in essential vitamins, minerals, proteins, fruits, and vegetables. A healthy diet doesn't just benefit your body—it has a profound impact on your mental health as well. The food you consume undergoes complex chemical processes in your body, releasing hormones and chemicals that support various functions. Eating nutrient-rich foods ensures the release of hormones that strengthen your body and mind, helping you recover more effectively over time.

2. **Limit Junk Food, but Indulge When Needed:** While it's important to avoid junk food, processed sugars, carbonated drinks, and frozen meals as much as possible, it's equally important to practice kindness toward yourself. If you're going through a particularly rough time, treating yourself to your favorite comfort food can offer a much-needed sense of relief and solace. Striking a balance is key—don't be overly strict about sticking to a diet. Occasional indulgences can help lift your spirits, and the effort to maintain this balance is what matters most on your recovery journey.

3. **Embrace the Journey, Ups, and Downs Included:** Recovery is rarely a straight path. There will be days when progress feels elusive, but it's important not to let setbacks discourage you. Each small victory brings you closer to transformation. Keep reminding yourself of your ultimate goal: building a healthier, more resilient version of yourself.

4. **Incorporate Medicinal Herbs and Spices:** Natural remedies can complement your recovery process. Add medicinal herbs and spices such as turmeric, lemon, ginger, garlic, ashwagandha, chamomile, lavender, and tulsi (holy basil) into your routine. Whether in teas, health drinks, or concoctions, these ingredients are known to alleviate stress, reduce anxiety and depression, stabilize mood,

and calm your senses. With consistent use, they can significantly enhance your overall health and well-being.
5. **Be Mindful of Caffeine:** If you notice that caffeine or tea exacerbates your restlessness or anxiety, it's best to reduce or avoid them. Opt for soothing alternatives such as lemonade, coconut water, chamomile tea, or ginger-lemon infusions. These beverages can help relax your mind and promote a sense of calm.
6. **Stay Hydrated and Experiment with Fasting:** Regular hydration is essential for maintaining optimal body function and regulating internal processes. Along with staying hydrated, consider fasting once a week. Fasting offers numerous health benefits, including naturally detoxifying your body and improving overall wellness. If a full day of fasting isn't feasible due to medical reasons, try spacing out your meals by 6–8 hours to achieve similar benefits.

8

Interdependence Among Dimensions of Well-Being

Everyone has a unique understanding of what health truly means. Someone might feel unwell despite having no physical signs or symptoms, while another person could feel completely in sync with optimal health despite living with a slowly progressing disease. Different health practitioners assess an individual's health based on the specific dimension of health they specialize in. For example, a general physician might declare a person healthy if they find no signs or symptoms of physical illness. However, a psychiatrist might arrive at a different conclusion based on their specialized area of diagnosis.

As you may already know, holistic health results from an ideal balance across all dimensions of existence. Every living being on this planet perceives life through various dimensions, shaped by their sensory experience of the self and the world. These dimensions can be broadly categorized as Physical, Mental, Emotional, Social, Environmental, Occupational, and Spiritual. One must strive for balance across all these dimensions to achieve a sense of holistic well-being.

These dimensions are deeply interconnected. If one or more are disrupted—by internal or external factors—it can disturb the delicate equilibrium of health. For instance, a physical ailment or injury can lead to emotional responses, affecting a person's mental or social well-being. The degree of this influence varies from person to person but is undeniable. Similarly, prolonged mental strain can manifest as psychosomatic symptoms, impacting an individual's physical health and emotional balance. Take, for example, someone with a history of anxiety or depression. This can slow reflexes, impair the functioning of internal organs, and lead to symptoms such as brain fog, blurred vision, vestibular issues, a rapid heartbeat, facial tension, and more. Understanding this interdependence allows us to use it to our advantage.

Now, let's specifically discuss **Depersonalization-Derealization Disorder (DPDR)**, which affects all dimensions of an individual's well-being—some more than others. By utilizing the concept of interdependence, one can work toward improving overall well-being over time. Below is a breakdown of how DPDR impacts the various dimensions of wellness:

- **Physical**: Individuals often experience symptoms such as blurred vision, brain fog, facial tension, slow reflexes, vestibular (balance) problems, persistent migraines, slurred speech, and eye floaters.
- **Mental**: Mentally, the individual is stuck in a constant fight-or-flight mode, leading to frequent panic attacks, persistent anxiety, intrusive thoughts, OCD, and sometimes

depression.
- **Emotional**: During peak phases, emotional numbness is common. Individuals may struggle to feel or express emotions, or they might experience heightened emotional vulnerability.
- **Social**: DPDR significantly impacts social life. It often leads to social anxiety and phobias like agoraphobia, where individuals avoid places or situations that might trigger panic. Many avoid social interactions entirely.
- **Occupational**: Constant symptoms and irrational thoughts make it challenging to focus on work. This lack of focus and divided attention negatively affects productivity and the quality of work delivered.
- **Spiritual**: For some, DPDR may feel like a spiritual awakening, though this perspective varies. The heightened awareness of self and surroundings often leads to existential questions, mental confusion, and emotional turmoil, disrupting spiritual wellness.

Now that we have an understanding of how DPDR affects the different dimensions of wellness, let's explore how to leverage this interdependence for recovery. By focusing on dimensions that are more within our control, we can create a ripple effect that positively influences others.

In cases of DPDR—or any mental illness, for that matter—it can feel impossible to control your mind or emotions. Trying to do so often backfires, worsening the situation and leaving a person feeling even more helpless. The mental and emotional dimensions of well-being seem entirely out of sync with the others. But the beauty of human existence lies in the body's innate ability to heal itself. Every symptom—whether physical or mental—is the body's way of signaling that something requires attention. When mental and emotional health feels beyond reach, redirecting focus to the physical dimension can be incredibly effective. By prioritizing simple actions like regular exercise, maintaining a healthy diet, or ensuring proper rest, one can begin to stabilize the mind and emotions. Over time, this stability extends to other dimensions, restoring balance and harmony across all aspects of existence.

Why do health practitioners consistently emphasize the importance of physical activity? Across the world, people—whether experts or not—understand the importance of staying active. Activities like strength training, yoga, aerobics, or even a simple daily walk provide unique and shared benefits that significantly enhance overall health. For those navigating mental health challenges like DPDR, physical activity can serve as a powerful tool. Movement doesn't just strengthen the body; it helps regulate the mind. Exercise releases endorphins, which naturally uplift your mood, and reduces stress hormones, helping to calm the nervous system. Physical effort helps foster a sense of control and progress. And it's not just the physical dimension that aids in DPDR. When you focus on one area, like engaging in a hobby or connecting with nature, it ripples into others. Emotional well-being grows through mindfulness and meaningful relationships. Pursuing work or activities that reflect your core values can give you purpose and stability, while spiritual practices like meditation quiet the mental noise. Even something as simple as cleaning your space or stepping outdoors can improve your outlook.

By addressing the areas you can control, you naturally support the ones that feel out of reach. With patience and consistency, these small efforts in various dimensions of your life work together to rebuild balance, offering hope and progress, even with conditions as challenging as DPDR.

9

Harnessing Nature's Tools for Healing

Depersonalization-Derealization Disorder (DPDR) can significantly impact an individual's well-being across various dimensions. As it often involves a detachment from oneself and the surrounding environment, it leads to distressing symptoms and challenges in daily life. However, incorporating various practices such as strength training, meditation, and yoga can provide significant benefits and support the overall healing process. These practices may not be a one-stop solution to dissociative disorders, but they definitely act as catalysts in recovering faster. These practices can positively impact individuals with DPDR by promoting physical, mental, and emotional well-being. It is extremely important for individuals with DPDR to experience a sense of safety and well-being with time to begin their healing journey.

Strength Training: As we know, it's a form of physical exercise aimed at building muscle strength and endurance, but it also offers several benefits for individuals with DPDR.

a. **Physical Benefits**: Engaging in regular strength training exercises can enhance physical well-being, leading to various improvements such as increased energy levels, improved sleep patterns, and enhanced overall physical health. Additionally, strength training helps release endorphins that act as natural painkillers and mood enhancers. They are released during exercise, stress, and pleasurable activities, contributing to feelings of well-being and reducing pain perception.

b. **Body Awareness**: DPDR often involves a disconnection from the physical body and immediate surroundings. Strength training also encourages individuals to develop a deeper connection with their bodies, fostering body awareness and grounding. By focusing on specific muscle groups and movements, individuals can cultivate a sense of embodiment, reducing dissociative symptoms. Through regular strength training sessions, affected individuals can rewire their neural connections with time to develop a sense of safety, calmness, and relaxation within themselves and their surroundings. This way, a constant sense of fear caused by irrational threats could be managed and reduced steadily.

c. **Empowerment and Confidence**: Strength training empowers individuals by setting achievable goals and experiencing progress over time. As individuals witness improvements in their physical strength and endurance, they also develop increased self-confidence and self-esteem. This newfound confidence can positively influence their overall perception of self and support their journey toward recovery. Along with that, an individual feels more connected with themselves as their thoughts align with the physical action brought upon by these thoughts, therefore redeveloping a connection with themselves.

Meditation: It involves training the mind to focus and redirect thoughts to reduce stress, anxiety, and experience relaxation. Several meditation techniques, such as mindfulness, can help DPDR-affected individuals gain a sense of control over their thoughts and emotions, which in turn can regulate their after-effects in the form of hormonal imbalance, adrenaline response, and psychosomatic symptoms.

a. **Mindfulness and Grounding**: As DPDR often involves a sense of detachment and disconnection, meditation techniques, particularly mindfulness, enable individuals to foster present-moment awareness and ground themselves in the here and now. By practicing regular mindfulness, individuals can learn to observe their thoughts and emotions without judgment, reducing dissociative tendencies and improving overall emotional regulation. As every individual's mind is continuously manufacturing big data of thoughts, it's crucial for us to identify and differentiate between rational and irrational thoughts, and not believe the irrational ones, which produce fear and "fight-or-flight" responses in our bodies, leading to panic attacks and other stressful responses.

b. **Stress Reduction**: Meditation is a powerful tool for stress reduction, which is particularly relevant for individuals with DPDR and other dissociative disorders who often experience heightened levels of anxiety and distress. Regular meditation practice can help individuals develop a greater capacity to manage stress, promoting a sense of calm and stability.

Individuals affected by DPDR need to understand that persistence is crucial over several weeks to notice significant positive changes in how they psychologically respond to both internal thoughts and external stimuli from their surroundings.

c. **Self-Reflection and Inner Exploration**: Meditation provides an opportunity for self-reflection and introspection, allowing individuals to explore their inner experiences and gain insights into their dissociative symptoms. By developing a deeper understanding of their thoughts and emotions, individuals can work toward healing and integration. Dissociative disorders lead to disintegration between all dimensions of health: physical, mental, emotional, and spiritual, whereas meditation has the potential to regain the lost balance and tune in the sync between these dimensions, which is extremely crucial for achieving a sense of overall well-being.

Yoga: It's a holistic practice that combines physical postures, breath control, and meditation. It offers numerous benefits for individuals with dissociative disorders, especially DPDR.

a. **Body-Mind Connection**: Yoga promotes the integration of body and mind, fostering a sense of unity and connection. Through the practice of yoga postures (asanas), individuals can cultivate body awareness, enhance physical flexibility, and improve overall body-mind coordination. This integration can help counteract dissociative tendencies and create a more harmonious sense of self. When an individual's body, thoughts, and spirit begin to harmonize and find balance within themselves over time through consistent training, feelings of depersonalization start to diminish, and they begin to regain their lost sense of self.

b. **Stress Relief and Relaxation**: Practicing yoga, especially gentle and restorative forms, can induce a state of deep relaxation, allowing individuals to release tension, reduce anxiety, and alleviate symptoms of dissociation. Yoga's emphasis on conscious breathing techniques (pranayama) such as Anuloma Vyloma (alternate nostril breath) and Brahmri (hummingbee breath) further produces relaxation and supports emotional well-being. These breathing exercises, when performed regularly in a controlled environment, have the potential to reboot the brain by enhancing its plasticity, soothing the nerves, and even improving sleep patterns over successive training sessions.

c. **Emotional Regulation and Self-Compassion**: Yoga also encourages individuals to cultivate a compassionate and non-judgmental attitude toward themselves. Through regular yoga, an individual with DPDR inches closer to a self-acceptance stage, which is the basis of recovery in DPDR. Self-acceptance and a letting-go attitude propel individuals to come out of obtrusive thought patterns, which significantly improves the condition with time.

Cardio Exercises: Aerobic or cardiovascular exercises focus on the large muscle groups within a short period in order to increase the heart rate by a significant jump, which offers a lot of health benefits both physically and mentally, more so in safeguarding the brain from further damage. As per scientific studies, high-intensity exercises such as cardio (dancing, running, jumping, etc.) increase Brain-derived Neurotrophic Factor (BDNF), which in turn supports learning and memory. Exercises in this area could greatly benefit individuals with DPDR by halting further deterioration of memory and plasticity, enhancing learning capabilities, and supporting the brain's rewiring by training to control the mind.

In Conclusion, incorporating strength training, meditation, yoga, and aerobic exercises into daily life can offer significant benefits to individuals seeking relief from their symptoms. These practices support physical well-being, promote body awareness, enhance emotional regulation, and provide tools for stress reduction and relaxation. Furthermore, these practices provide a foundation for DPDR-affected individuals to redevelop a sense of familiarity and connection with themselves and their environment, enabling them to re-associate their thoughts, body, mind, soul, and surroundings as a unified whole.

10

Mindful Distraction: A Path to Temporary Solace

For individuals experiencing DPDR for the first time, it can be a profoundly unsettling experience. They struggle to process these unfamiliar and undesirable sensations, often finding themselves in a perpetual state of internal fight-or-flight. This only amplifies the intensity of depersonalized and derealized feelings. It's an entirely new, unwanted experience—one that brings extreme terror and disrupts the brain's ability to process information effectively, triggered by both external and internal stimuli.

For those who have lived with DPDR for a while, they eventually learn to manage their thoughts, feelings, and emotions. Over time, they find ways to reduce their focus on symptoms, enabling them to function in their personal and professional lives while experiencing fewer panic episodes than they did initially.

It is vital for those new to DPDR to understand how to manage their symptoms, thoughts, and emotions effectively to ensure that their personal, professional, and social lives remain as unaffected as possible. Mental health challenges, whether hypochondria, schizophrenia, bipolar disorder, or DPDR, have the potential to disrupt every facet of life, often resulting in a vicious cycle of declining mental health. Equipping oneself with the right tools and techniques to navigate these challenges can help calm the mind, provide temporary solace during distress, and build resilience over time. This brings up an important question: how can one consciously achieve a sense of calm and peace while feeling overwhelmed by the misery that DPDR brings?

Distraction is a powerful yet often overlooked tool for managing DPDR. Many individuals mistakenly believe that focusing on their symptoms and thoughts will help them overcome the disorder. However, this approach frequently backfires, leading to deeper involvement in their suffering. Constant rumination over intrusive thoughts and symptoms strengthens their grip, making the depersonalized state more persistent and intense. This cycle often lasts weeks or months for those newly diagnosed with DPDR. Over time, the subconscious mind adapts, perceiving the distorted reality of DPDR as a new and unchanging truth.

Engaging in distraction, in any form, is crucial for breaking this cycle. Activities that demand mental and physical involvement create a much-needed sense of safety and temporary relief from intrusive thoughts and emotional turmoil. Work, leisure pursuits, or rekindling old hobbies can be great starting points. Listening to music, playing sports, watching movies, spending time with pets, or even tidying up your living space are effective ways to shift your focus. Though it may feel unnatural at first—given the negative emotions like guilt or regret—you must persevere. Intrusive thoughts and psychological distress may persist, but consistently engaging in these activities will gradually help you reconnect with the parts of life you once enjoyed.

Additionally, learning new skills or trying novel activities can have profound benefits. These endeavors not only distract the mind but also stimulate the brain to form new neural pathways, improving cognitive function and memory. For example, picking up a musical instrument, learning a new language, or experimenting with creative outlets like painting or writing can revitalize the mind and body. By doing so, you create a buffer for yourself—a mental space that allows for rest and renewal.

Keeping your mind engaged is one of the most effective ways to reassociate with life and regain a sense of normalcy. Activities that require active participation and focus help ground you in the present moment and rebuild the connection to your surroundings. For instance, joining a group activity like yoga, hiking, or volunteering can provide not only a structured distraction but also opportunities for social interaction and support. Gardening, cooking, or even assembling puzzles are small yet meaningful ways to channel your energy into something constructive. By consistently engaging in such activities, you allow yourself to break free from the grip of DPDR and gradually reintegrate into a fulfilling and balanced life.

11

Six Weeks of Healing and Growth

Everyone suffering from depersonalization longs to recover as quickly as possible. However, only a few have the courage to follow the right path and take the necessary actions. Instead of placing faith in the misconceptions of others or seeking an easy fix through medications or procedures—none of which are specifically designed to treat this disorder—it's crucial to recognize that recovery comes to those who not only desire it but also understand the steps required to make meaningful progress over time.

We must break free from the cobweb of the problem—the depersonalized and derealized state of living—and start identifying practical options to reclaim the life we deserve. Seeking professional help and using prescribed medications to support recovery can undoubtedly provide relief and accelerate the process. However, relying solely on these tools without taking proactive steps of your own will not lead to true healing. Recovery requires effort, resilience, and an active commitment to change.

Every disease in this world stems from causes that may be genetic, environmental, due to deficiencies, or psychological or physiological in nature. Some are curable, while others are not; certain chronic conditions can be managed with medications and therapies, whereas others demand surgical intervention due to their severity. However, it's crucial to understand that recovery, in large part, hinges on the individual's own actions and mindset. While medical support is indispensable, an individual's choices and conduct play a significant role in accelerating recovery. Choosing a healthy lifestyle over convenient or popular preferences can dramatically enhance the healing process. These choices—encompassing diet, exercise or physical activity, sleep habits, stress management, and work-life balance—are far from easy. They demand discipline, courage, sincerity, and unwavering faith in oneself to sustain the effort and achieve long-term success. The same principle applies to mental health. Mental illnesses, when endured for extended periods, can lead to serious physiological effects, making it vital to prioritize consistent progress. By committing to better habits and taking deliberate steps forward, individuals can create a foundation for positive outcomes and lasting well-being.

Recovering from depersonalization-derealization largely depends on the affected individual's sheer willpower and commitment to healing. With the support of professional assistance—such as behavioral therapy and psychiatric medications to restore chemical balance—an individual can make significant progress over time and achieve remarkable recovery if they are willing to do whatever it takes to break free from the dissociative state marked by fear, agony, and despair. Although positive changes may not be immediately noticeable, maintaining consistency is crucial to experiencing long-term benefits. A DPDR-affected individual must exercise strict discipline in key aspects of their life, including diet and nutrition, physical activity, sleep routines, relationships, and career, to propel their recovery forward. Sacrificing short-term gratifications for long-term health and well-being is a timeless principle—one that never loses its value. By giving up temporary comforts, individuals position themselves to reap the desirable rewards of a healthier future. It's equally important to acknowledge that abruptly abandoning unhealthy habits is often counterproductive. Such drastic changes can lead to unexpected setbacks or frequent relapses. Instead, adopting a tapering approach—gradually reducing old habits while incorporating healthier ones—allows for a more sustainable and effective transformation. This method not only minimizes the likelihood of backtracking but also fosters a smoother transition to a healthier and more balanced way of life. The below Six Weeks Recovery Guide is meant to support individuals in advancing their recovery process and help them retrain their subconscious responses to themselves and their surroundings:

Week 1: Acceptance and Distraction

Acceptance is the crucial first step in the recovery journey. It involves coming to terms with the fact that our condition is beyond our immediate control. The more we try to control it, the stronger it holds onto our subconscious. The goal is to stop resisting this condition and instead take small steps to move forward with life, even while still experiencing the undesirable feelings it brings.

Below is an example of how you can begin to accept your condition and take gradual steps to re-engage with other areas of your life:

Affirmation: *"Yes, I have Depersonalization and Derealization. The symptoms cause me anxiety and depression, but there's not much I can do to fix this immediately. However, I am capable of living my life by focusing on different areas, even while feeling dissociated. Instead of wallowing in self-pity, I can channel the same energy into my work and activities I once enjoyed. While these may not bring the same feelings as before, they will provide a sense of nostalgia—a feeling closest to the life I had before dissociation overtook me."*

Repeat this affirmation to yourself over the next few days. With each repetition, you will build confidence and start taking action in other important areas of your life. This practice will help you shift from the cycle of self-pity and begin embracing acceptance.

Distraction Facilitates Acceptance

Distraction plays a key role in making acceptance easier. While repeating the affirmation in your mind is a powerful first step, it won't be fully effective unless you begin to move from your current mindset to a more receptive one. This shift can be achieved through intentional distractions. Distractions are activities that capture your attention and invoke positive emotions, overriding intrusive thoughts. As you focus on accepting your condition, intentionally engage in activities you enjoy. Many people lose touch with their hobbies after being diagnosed with this disorder, but reconnecting with these activities—however difficult it may seem—can be immensely helpful. If you once enjoyed watching movies, listening to music, dancing, gardening, reading, playing sports, or video games, try incorporating these into your routine more often. Even if they don't provide the same joy as before, they will serve as a powerful distraction and help you reconnect with life. *Trust me, these small steps will guide you through the process of moving forward.*

Week 2:

Mindfulness and Affirmation with Continued Acceptance and Distraction

Once you've made progress in practicing Acceptance and Distraction during the first week, it's time to build on that foundation with the next step: incorporating Mindfulness and Affirmations, while continuing with Acceptance and Distraction as before. For many of us with DPDR, there's a tendency to get trapped in irrational thoughts, backed by an altered perception of reality. These thoughts often lead to severe mental distress and intense psychosomatic symptoms. While Acceptance and Distraction in the first week help lay the groundwork for recovery, there comes a point where minimal progress will be made unless we address the root cause of our issues. Therefore, it's crucial to continue practicing Acceptance and Distraction but also to introduce mindfulness and positive affirmations into your daily life. There's an abundance of mindfulness techniques available online, and countless professionals offer classes to help develop this skill. Learning to observe your thoughts without immediately believing them may take time, but even a 70% mastery of this skill will make the rest of your recovery journey much easier.

Mindfulness:

Mindfulness can be practiced at any moment—whether you're working, sleeping, or simply sitting idle. Our minds are constantly flooded with thoughts, even during deep sleep, so instead of reacting to them instinctively, try to observe them from a third-person perspective. Let the thoughts pass like visitors, and reflect on their root cause. Ask yourself: *What triggered these thoughts? Are they based on past experiences or fears about the future?* For example, imagine you're thinking: *"I'm losing my sanity; everything around me feels magnified and unreal. My body parts don't seem to belong to me, and I feel like I'm floating outside myself."* These thoughts often trigger your fight-or-flight response, causing anxiety or panic. Now, observe how you feel over the next hour or the rest of the day. Ask yourself: *"Did I really lose my sanity as I feared? Did I go crazy? Did my surroundings change, or did my body parts detach from me?"*

By consistently questioning your irrational thoughts, you'll start to see patterns in your thinking. Mindfulness isn't a one-time activity, but a continual practice. Over time, you'll gain more control over your thoughts and start to trust them less. While you may not see significant progress right away, keep practicing—this skill will pave the way for greater mental well-being.

Meditation and Positive Affirmations:

Meditation is the practice of focusing on the present moment.

Our minds have an incredible ability to wander, often revisiting the past or worrying about the future. With DPDR, it's common for our thoughts to bounce between time periods, creating a sense of disorientation. Meditation helps train your mind to notice when it's drifting and gently brings your focus back to the present. Choose something simple to focus on—a point in the room, your breath, or even your own presence—and, each time your mind drifts, kindly guide it back to your point of focus. This brain training exercise helps you regain control over your thoughts, allowing you to maintain a steady focus on the present rather than allowing your thoughts to run wild. Alongside mindfulness, you should practice positive affirmations to reinforce healthier thinking. Even when negative thoughts arise, combat them with affirmations, no matter how unrealistic they may seem at first. Over time, you'll notice a shift—replacing negative thoughts with positive affirmations will help you build mental strength and resilience.

Example of Positive Affirmations:

Intrusive thoughts might sound like: *"I'll never recover from this dreadful condition. I'll lose my sanity because of DPDR. I can't take it anymore. There's no hope! I can't even go to work or out for groceries because I feel overwhelmed by everything around me."*

Instead, replace them with positive affirmations: *"I will recover from DPDR, just as many others have. If I've managed to survive this long with DPDR, I won't lose my sanity. I've endured this for so long, and I'll continue to grow stronger. I will stay hopeful and committed to my recovery. Even though it's challenging, I will keep working while experiencing DPDR, because it's difficult but not impossible. I will step out of my comfort zone and go shopping, and I will keep doing it until I feel more at ease in social situations, even if I feel overwhelmed."*

Repeat these affirmations as often as you can. The more you practice, the more you'll begin to see real progress in your healing journey. Positive affirmations offer a much-needed sense of catharsis, reinforcing your commitment to recovery and your belief in yourself.

Week 3:

Using Psychological Tools to Alleviate Psychosomatic Symptoms

After the first two weeks of coming to terms with your condition through Acceptance, and progressing with powerful techniques like Distraction, Mindfulness, and Positive Affirmations, all of which primarily focus on the mental aspect of your well-being, it's time to expand our approach to include other dimensions for holistic recovery. While the mind plays a central role in your healing journey, the physical body is equally important. As we've discussed the interconnectedness of different aspects of human existence, it's clear that mental struggles can manifest physically, and vice versa. In the case of dissociation, such as depersonalization-derealization, a range of psychosomatic symptoms can arise as a response to the affected mental state. These symptoms often feel just as real and distressing as physical ailments, even though they may not show up in a physician's examination. Conditions like Anxiety, Depression, Panic Attacks, and Dissociation are not only mental but also deeply physical. Anxiety may manifest in symptoms like shortness of breath, sweaty palms, or nausea. Panic attacks bring about palpitations and the sensation of losing consciousness. Depression and Dissociation often lead to brain fog, blurred vision, and slower reflexes.

Given this, it's vital to address these physical manifestations through psychological tools and techniques that can help you manage and overcome them, making significant progress toward recovery. Below are the techniques I used to alleviate the psychosomatic symptoms I experienced:

Conscious Multitasking: Multitasking is an effective way to keep your mind engaged in various activities, reducing space for intrusive thoughts. Switching between different tasks, whether similar or not, helps distract the mind from dissociative symptoms and refocuses it on accomplishing tasks. This active engagement challenges the brain and can help build mental resilience and stability over time. For example, switching between working on a project and reading an article, doing household chores simultaneously, or talking to someone on the phone while taking a walk can be powerful ways to occupy your mind. It's important to note, though, that multitasking might not be suitable for everyone. For some, it can lead to stress or exhaustion. There's no harm in trying this technique, but if you feel overwhelmed, adjust the intensity or frequency to suit your needs.

Subconscious Division of Attention: Unlike multitasking, which requires active attention, the subconscious division of attention involves engaging both passive and active activities simultaneously. A dissociated mind can be hyperactive, constantly absorbing the smallest details of its surroundings, while also being preoccupied with physical symptoms. Dividing your attention between two or more tasks that require both active and passive involvement can help reduce the mind's tendency to overthink and focus on distressing thoughts or symptoms. By doing this, you allow the subconscious to spread its attention, minimizing hypervigilance and reducing overall anxiety. This can also help prevent panic attacks and lessen the intensity of dissociation. People affected by DPDR can benefit from this technique by applying it during work or other important tasks. Here are a few examples of how this can be done:

- **Chewing gum and listening to music while sleeping:** By engaging in these two passive activities (chewing gum and listening to music), you divide the subconscious mind's focus, making it harder for intrusive thoughts to dominate your mental space during sleep.
- **Listening to music, singing, and exercising at the same time during a workout:** Here, you're combining two passive activities (listening to music and singing) with an active one (exercising). This combination creates a "mental buffer" for the dissociated person, leaving little room for negative thoughts or physical discomforts during that time.

This approach to managing psychosomatic symptoms will allow you to maintain focus and build resilience as you continue your journey to recovery. By leveraging both conscious and subconscious techniques, you can gradually alleviate the intensity of your experiences and foster a healthier balance between the mental and physical aspects of healing.

Week 4:

Learning and Development

You may be wondering how learning and development could possibly help in recovering from dissociation—it might not seem to make much sense at first. However, it's important to understand that learning isn't a one-time fix to eliminate DPDR from your life, but rather a powerful tool that can support your recovery throughout your entire journey. Continuous learning plays a key role in maintaining and improving brain health through neuroplasticity. This process helps strengthen existing neural pathways and form new ones, a phenomenon that continues throughout life. By keeping your brain active and engaged, learning supports the maintenance of cognitive functions, which are crucial in everyday life.

With Depersonalization-Derealization Disorder (DPDR), cognitive decline often accompanies the condition, manifesting as symptoms like blurred vision, slower reflexes, floaters, and hyperacusis. These cognitive challenges can worsen over time, but the good news is that they can be mitigated through continuous learning and development. Whether it's learning a new professional skill, picking up a new language, reading books, solving puzzles, or even exploring new places and meeting new people, all of these activities contribute to not only improving your mental health but also boosting your brain's overall well-being during your recovery. Beyond cognitive improvement, learning something new also gives you a sense of control.

Mastering a new skill requires full attention and focus, which helps divert your mind from overthinking about your symptoms. It breaks the cycle of repetitive, disturbing thoughts that cause emotional and physical pain.

That being said, learning new skills isn't always easy—especially when DPDR is always lingering in the background. It takes a lot of motivation and mental effort to push through the resistance and dedicate yourself to learning. Your dissociated mind will often try to distract you, pulling your attention back to your symptoms and thoughts. But this is where mindfulness comes in. You can practice thinking of learning as a distraction from the obsessive cycle of thoughts about your condition. It may take time and persistence, but every effort, no matter how small, helps rewire your brain and strengthens your resolve on the path to recovery.

Remember, recovery is a journey, and learning—whether it's a new skill, a book, or a puzzle—is an ongoing tool to support your mental health and growth. Keep practicing, and over time, you'll notice improvements that go beyond just learning—they'll show up in how you feel mentally and physically too.

Week 5:

Sensory Consumption and Lifestyle Changes

What you consume and how you live your life have a significant impact on your health. This goes beyond just what you eat—it also includes everything you experience through your senses. The food you eat is undeniably important as it forms the foundation of your physical health, but other senses, like sight, sound, and touch, are just as influential in shaping your mental and emotional well-being. The content you consume—whether it's what you read, watch, or listen to—directly impacts your mind. Because of this, it's essential to be conscious of all forms of consumption in your life.

Beyond sensory consumption, lifestyle choices also play a crucial role in fostering overall health. There's no shortage of advice online about how healthy habits can transform your life. Whether it's regular exercise, a consistent sleep schedule, eating the right foods based on your climate, or maintaining good hygiene, every small habit contributes to your holistic well-being. Even a 1% improvement in various areas can add up, leading to a 10% improvement in your overall health.

Food: Your diet has a profound influence not only on your physical health but also on your mental, emotional, and spiritual well-being. Eating healthy, nutritious food isn't just great for your body—it can also improve your mood by releasing feel-good chemicals like dopamine. For those on a spiritual journey, certain foods, like sattvik (pure) foods, are believed to enhance mental clarity and vitality due to their purity and lightness. However, with Depersonalization-Derealization (DPDR), it's important not to take extreme dietary approaches, as this can backfire and worsen your condition. The goal should be to cultivate a balanced sense of well-being while also finding joy in what you eat. Many people struggling with mental health issues swing between extreme dietary choices—some may avoid all unhealthy foods, like sugar and junk, while others might indulge in them excessively to experience temporary relief. Both approaches tend to cause more harm than good in the long run, leading to relapses and worsening physical health.

So, with DPDR, aim for a balanced diet that fosters both health and happiness. Here's a simple guideline:

- Keep 80% of your diet healthy and clean, including foods that provide wholesome nutrition and fulfill your body's chemical needs (like B vitamins, Vitamin C, D, A, K, and important minerals like zinc, magnesium, and selenium).
- Include antioxidants to fight inflammation caused by free radicals.
- Caffeine should be consumed in moderation—limit yourself to 1 or 2 cups a day. If caffeine tends to heighten anxiety for you, it's best to avoid it.
- Refreshing drinks like lemonade, coconut water, beetroot juices, and even occasional fruit juices can help you feel revitalized and calm.

Allow yourself to enjoy the remaining 20% of your diet by indulging in your favorite comfort food or snack. Don't feel guilty—eating in moderation provides mental pleasure, boosts mood, and can help stabilize your mental state.

Content: When it comes to content consumption, make mindful choices. As someone living with a condition that's often misunderstood, it's crucial to understand DPDR thoroughly. Educate yourself by reading trustworthy material and engaging with support groups where you can both share and receive encouragement. However, many individuals with DPDR can fall into the trap of obsessively consuming negative stories or horror stories of people who haven't recovered, which only increases hopelessness. This negative spiral does more harm than good, so it's important to limit your engagement with such content once you've gained the necessary knowledge. Also, it's natural for those with DPDR to feel drawn to sad movies, emotional music, or other content that mirrors their mood. While this is a subconscious coping mechanism, it moves you further from your ultimate goal of healing. Try to become aware of this tendency and make efforts to bring more positive content into your life.

Solution: Do the opposite of what you're feeling. If you're anxious, sad, or hopeless, consume content that brings hope and positivity into your life. Listen to cheerful music, watch uplifting movies, or read books that inspire confidence and remind you of your strength. One of the most powerful tools for recovery is humor. Trust me—laughter is truly the best medicine. It eases psychological pain and relieves exhaustion when the recovery journey feels overwhelming. Never underestimate the power of laughter in healing. Make it a non-negotiable part of your routine.

Week 6:

Expanding Involvement in Other Dimensions

By now, you've already started your healing journey, primarily focusing on the mental and physical dimensions of well-being. However, to achieve true holistic recovery, it's essential to bring other aspects of your being into focus. As we've discussed repeatedly, a balanced life is the key to well-being, and this balance must include the mental, physical, social, environmental, occupational, and spiritual dimensions. Recovery is not complete until all of these areas are actively nurtured.

The following pointers will help you understand how engaging with these dimensions positively impacts your mental and physical health:

Social Wellness: Social connections play a critical role in improving mental health. By staying connected to family, friends, and communities, you create a sense of belonging. This fosters trust, emotional support, and empathy—essential components of wellness. Interacting with others can alleviate feelings of loneliness and anxiety, lift your spirits, and boost overall mental well-being. Engaging socially brings you into a network where you can both give and receive support, which is essential for managing DPDR and overall life improvement.

Environmental Wellness: Exposure to the world outside your home, especially when dealing with DPDR, can be daunting. However, stepping into real-world environments, no matter how overwhelming they may seem initially, is crucial for your recovery. Gradually familiarizing yourself with different settings and situations will help you regain trust in your surroundings and reduce the fear that exacerbates your condition. At first, you may feel anxious and notice every detail around you, but over time, these sensations will decrease, and you'll develop a sense of comfort and ease. If the intensity of perception becomes too much, wearing darker sunglasses or shades can help reduce visual overwhelm, helping you stay calm as you acclimate.

Occupational Wellness: DPDR can significantly impact your work life. Difficulty focusing and reduced productivity often accompany this condition, which may affect your professional life. The anxiety about falling behind or facing judgment can increase your stress levels and hinder recovery. However, by addressing occupational wellness—maintaining your focus, staying organized, and managing your career—you contribute positively to both your mental health and overall recovery. A stable work life provides a sense of purpose, routine, and accomplishment, which is vital for long-term healing.

Spiritual Wellness: The spiritual dimension is deeply intertwined with mental health. Spiritual wellness is about finding meaning and purpose in life, especially when dealing with existential questions that often arise with DPDR. Practices like mindfulness, meditation, and yoga help develop spiritual awareness, providing insights into your life's purpose and the greater universe. Many individuals with DPDR experience an existential crisis, questioning their identity, purpose, and the nature of life itself. However, spiritual practices can guide you through these uncertainties, improving self-awareness, self-esteem, and emotional regulation. This awareness can lead to profound healing, as it connects you with the innate ability of your body and mind to recover. Your inner wisdom, when nurtured, can unlock natural healing mechanisms and aid in your recovery.

At the end of this chapter, I want to share my firm belief that if you follow this "Six-Week Recovery Guide" consistently, it will bring about lasting transformation in your life. While I'm not claiming it will be a miracle cure that erases DPDR entirely, it will lead to a substantial improvement—likely by 50%. This progress is significant. And if you continue these practices after the six-week period, your recovery will keep advancing. Over the next few months, you will find yourself emerging from the depths of DPDR and returning to the vibrant, happy life you deserve. You've been through so much, and now it's time to heal fully and live the life you've always been worthy of.

12

Everyday Tools to Support Your Healing

Practical Tools for Coping with DPDR

Wearing Shades: In Depersonalization-Derealization Disorder (DPDR), sensory perception can be heightened, leading to an overwhelming sense of threat. Wearing darker sunglasses or tinted eyeglasses can help alleviate this by reducing the intensity of magnified perceptions. This simple tool can calm your mind and create an additional layer of comfort when you're exposed to intense lighting, crowded spaces, or large structures—situations that often feel threatening to someone with DPDR. These shades can offer significant relief by soothing the panic response triggered by heightened sensory awareness.

Noise-Cancellation Headphones: Sounds in the environment can often seem distorted or amplified, triggering anxiety and panic. Noise-canceling headphones or earphones can help by blocking out these overwhelming sounds, creating a sense of calm and safety. However, it's important not to overuse them, as prolonged use may increase the risk of developing tinnitus, which can also be distressing.

Practicing Gratitude: Gratitude is a powerful, simple tool for shifting your mindset. By acknowledging and appreciating the positive aspects of your life—no matter how small—they can help you reconnect with hope and motivation. Incorporate gratitude into your daily routine, whether it's the first thing you do when you wake up or a moment of reflection at any point during your day. Consistent gratitude practice can provide a positive shift in perspective and contribute to your healing.

Listening to Cheerful Music: When you're feeling low, it can be tempting to listen to music that matches your mood, but uplifting and cheerful songs can be far more effective. Even when you're not in the mood, cheerful music helps elevate your emotional state and promotes a sense of tranquility. It's a simple, accessible way to lift your spirits and counter the heaviness of DPDR.

Chewing a Gum: While it may sound trivial, chewing gum can help redirect your subconscious mind, reducing anxiety and allowing you to focus less on intrusive thoughts. Chewing gum, particularly sugar-free, herb-flavored varieties, can be a simple yet effective tool for improving focus and reducing the intensity of psychosomatic symptoms. Try chewing for an hour, three times a day, to experience noticeable improvements over time.

Developing Selflessness and Practicing Kindness: Acts of kindness, especially when you're struggling yourself, can produce positive emotional benefits. Practicing selflessness not only increases feel-good chemicals in the brain but also fosters a sense of purpose. Even small gestures—helping others, offering support, or volunteering—can bring a sense of joy and satisfaction. Performing acts of kindness can counter the emotional numbness often caused by DPDR, providing a boost to both your mental health and sense of connection.

Raising a Pet or Caring for Strays: Caring for a pet or providing for stray animals can be an incredible source of emotional fulfillment, especially for those who find it difficult to connect with others. While raising a pet is a responsibility, it can also be a profound source of unconditional love and companionship. For those unable to commit to a pet, helping stray animals can offer similar benefits—creating a bond of love and reducing stress levels. Caring for animals provides both emotional and physical benefits, contributing to an overall sense of well-being.

Physical Labor: Engaging in physical activity is one of the most beneficial things you can do for both your body and mind. Regular exercise, yoga, strength training, dancing, or even doing household chores can have a powerful, positive impact on your mental health. It helps you stay grounded, builds strength, and fosters a sense of accomplishment. Just be mindful not to overexert yourself, as balance is key to maintaining a healthy routine.

13

Effective Ways to Manage DPDR Symptoms

As we are aware, Depersonalization-Derealization (DPDR) generates a variety of unpleasant feelings due to its characteristic symptoms, such as constant panic, a heavy sensation around the head, and visual disturbances like floaters. Experiencing these symptoms over an extended period can take a significant toll on a person's mental health and impair every aspect of life—whether personal, professional, social, or occupational. Recovering from DPDR is a unique journey for each individual, as it is influenced by many factors that vary from person to person. However, one crucial point is that recovery becomes much more challenging if individuals don't learn how to effectively manage their symptoms over time.

The key to easing the suffering caused by DPDR lies in learning to manage the psychosomatic symptoms. This management can make the recovery process less excruciating and more manageable. It is important to understand that these symptoms are not merely physical, but also affect mental, emotional, and spiritual well-being. This multifaceted disruption significantly interferes with daily life, as individuals with DPDR often just want relief from the constant discomfort in order to resume their normal activities.

Common Symptoms of DPDR:

DPDR manifests through a wide range of symptoms, affecting different dimensions of an individual's life. Below is a list of commonly experienced symptoms, categorized by their impact:

- **Psychosomatic Symptoms**: Palpitations, panic attacks, nausea, blurred vision, vertigo, floaters in the eyes, heavy-headedness, facial tension, muscle spasms, orthostatic hypotension (drop in blood pressure upon standing), tremors, balance disorders, disturbance in the body's natural sleep cycle, and more.
- **Psychological Symptoms**: Intrusive thoughts, hypochondria (health anxiety), generalized anxiety, depression, the sensation of floating or being out of one's body, time distortion (feeling like time is either moving too fast or too slow), perceiving intense surrounding noise, tinnitus, mental confusion, memory loss, fear of losing one's sanity, and more.
- **Emotional Symptoms**: Emotional numbness, detachment from one's feelings, emotional instability, bipolar tendencies (euphoric and depressive episodes), hysterical episodes, frequent mood swings, and more.
- **Spiritual Symptoms**: Questioning the meaning of life, the nature of the Universe, experiencing an existential crisis, heightened curiosity about life and death, spiritual

awakenings, and more.
- **Occupational Symptoms**: Distraction from work, lack of concentration, irritability, poor memory, issues with interpersonal communication, and more.
- **Social Symptoms**: Avoiding social gatherings, losing touch with relatives or friends, decreased bonding with family members, social anxiety, claustrophobia, and more.

As illustrated, the variety of symptoms experienced with DPDR is endless, and eliminating them overnight is simply not possible. However, accepting one's current state and making a conscious effort to manage these symptoms from the very beginning is key to regaining control of one's life. Without learning how to manage these symptoms, DPDR can gradually make a person feel as though they are losing control over themselves, leading to a heightened sense of detachment and a surreal existence.

Managing Symptoms: Practical Tips for Relief

Below are some practical, step-by-step tips for managing some of the most commonly experienced symptoms of DPDR. These strategies can help alleviate suffering and make it easier to carry on with daily chores and activities.

Eye Floaters: While eye floaters may be related to an underlying medical condition, a medical eye examination is important to rule out any issues. If tests are negative, using eye drops regularly can help alleviate strain. Splash cold water on your eyes several times a day, or gently rub your fingertips together and place them over your closed eyelids to soothe tired eyes. Wearing tinted sunglasses in bright or harsh-lit environments can reduce discomfort caused by eye strain.

Blurred Vision: Adequate sleep is crucial. If you experience insomnia, try taking short naps throughout the day to rest your brain and eyes. Reducing processed sugar intake is also beneficial, as high sugar consumption is linked to brain fog and blurry vision. Yoga and regular exercise will promote better blood flow to the brain and eyes, helping improve clarity of vision.

Panic Attacks: Mindfulness is an effective tool for managing panic. Find a comfortable, safe space to sit and focus your attention on the present moment. Engage in controlled breathing exercises to calm your mind and body. Other grounding techniques, such as focusing on your surroundings or physical sensations, can help keep you in the present. If these techniques do not work, consulting a psychiatrist may be helpful for exploring lightweight anti-anxiety medications for short-term relief.

Depression: DPDR and depression are often intertwined. One condition can exacerbate the other, and untreated depression can trigger or worsen DPDR symptoms. While medications can play a role, long-term recovery requires consistent effort in various aspects of life—career, health, relationships, and financial well-being. While DPDR and depression cannot be entirely "cured" with medications alone, making gradual progress in all areas of life can lead to substantial improvements—perhaps a 20-40% improvement in how you feel and function.

Out-of-Body Feeling: This symptom, though not experienced by everyone, can be unsettling when it occurs. It may feel like you are floating outside of your body or feeling unusually heavy. This feeling may be triggered by a panic attack, intense anxiety, or a chemical imbalance in the brain. Slow, deep breathing exercises like Nadi Shodhana (alternate nostril breathing) can help calm your mind and alleviate the feeling. Mindfulness practices and engaging in activities that distract your focus can also help manage these episodes.

Nausea: When nausea strikes, drinking cold water can offer immediate relief. Pair this with deep breathing exercises to simulate a sense of calm and ease the heightened anxiety that often accompanies nausea. Engage in distraction techniques, such as reading, watching calming videos, or listening to soothing music. Avoid caffeinated and sugary drinks, and opt for a fresh glass of lemonade with a squeeze of ginger juice, known for its anti-nausea properties.

Existential Crisis Worries: Existential thoughts can be overwhelming for those with DPDR, as they may start perceiving these philosophical concerns as threats. To break this cycle, use distraction to shift your focus away from these thoughts. Engage in an activity that captures your attention, whether it be a hobby, work, or a creative pursuit. Alternatively, mindfulness techniques can help you acknowledge your thoughts without becoming overly absorbed by them.

Vertigo: Vertigo may be caused by a medical condition, but if medical tests come back normal, it's likely the result of mental and emotional exhaustion from prolonged anxiety and DPDR. This can cause balance issues and light-headedness. Regular yoga, breathing exercises, and power naps are essential for restoring balance and mental clarity. Cardio exercises can further improve circulation to the brain and enhance overall cognitive function.

While there are many other common and rare symptoms associated with DPDR, most of them are manageable with a combination of physical exercises, dietary changes, and lifestyle choices. Over time, learning to manage symptoms can build confidence and accelerate recovery. With patience and persistence, individuals can significantly reduce their suffering and regain a sense of control over their lives.

14

The Power of Healing and Hope

As we come to the close of this journey together, I want to pause and recognize the immense strength it takes to walk the path of recovery from depersonalization and derealization (DPDR). You've faced a reality that is unfamiliar, often unsettling, and sometimes feels like an endless loop of confusion and detachment. Yet, here you are, at this point, seeking understanding and tools to regain control over your life—and that in itself is a powerful victory.

The journey of healing from DPDR is not one that happens overnight, and there are no shortcuts to regaining your sense of self. There will be moments where the symptoms feel unbearable, where it seems like the world around you is too distant to touch, and where every part of you longs for a sense of normalcy that seems just out of reach. But in those moments, I want you to remember: **healing is possible**.

Recovery doesn't come with a map, and it doesn't follow a clear-cut formula. It's different for each individual because each person's experience with DPDR is unique. There will be days when the fog of dissociation feels heavy and impenetrable. But with each step you take towards healing, that fog begins to clear. And one day, you will look back and realize how far you've come. The symptoms that once consumed your thoughts will no longer dictate your every move. You will have learned to live alongside them, without letting them control your life.

The key to healing lies not in the absence of symptoms, but in how we choose to respond to them. You don't need to be perfect, and you don't need to be symptom-free to live a fulfilling, meaningful life. What matters is your ability to manage those symptoms, to understand them, and to reclaim your space in the world. Every effort you make, no matter how small it may seem, brings you closer to a version of yourself that is stronger, more present, and more in control.

I understand that there will be times when the road seems uncertain when you question whether things will ever get better. It's okay to feel those doubts, to experience those moments of fear and frustration. What's important is that you don't let them define you. **You are not your symptoms.** They do not have the power to take away your worth, your purpose, or your ability to live a meaningful life. The power to heal lies within you, and with every step, you are taking back control, one small moment at a time.

Healing isn't a destination; it's a journey. There will be setbacks, there will be days when progress feels slow, but remember that **healing is not about perfection**. It's about progress. It's about showing up for yourself, every single day, even when it feels difficult. And bit by bit, you will start to notice shifts—small moments where the world feels a little more real, a little more grounded. Where the symptoms don't feel so overwhelming, and your sense of self begins to return. **That is progress**. That is healing.

I want you to know that you are not alone on this path. There is a vast community of people who understand what you're going through, people who have walked this journey before you and are now living lives full of purpose and meaning. You are part of a collective of resilient individuals who refuse to let their struggles define their lives. You are not isolated, and you don't have to face this alone.

It's also important to remember that recovery is never linear. There will be good days, and there will be challenging ones. But every day that you continue to make the choice to heal is a day you are taking back your life. **And that is something truly remarkable**.

In your healing, there is a power that comes from within—one that grows with every choice you make, every effort you put forth, and every moment you reclaim your peace. The magic of healing is that it doesn't happen all at once; it happens in the quiet moments, the small wins, and the daily choices to continue moving forward. **You are healing**. It's happening, even when you don't see it. And when you look back, you will realize just how far you've come.

So, as you move forward on this journey, remember this: **you are worthy of healing**. You are worthy of peace, of happiness, of a life where the symptoms no longer hold you back. Trust in the process. Trust in your ability to heal. Trust in the time it takes and the progress you make. You are stronger than you think, and the future is brighter than it may seem right now.

Healing is not just about recovery—it's about transformation. And in that transformation, you will find yourself again. You will find your power. You will find your peace. And you will find a life that is worth living. Keep believing in yourself, and never forget that you are never alone in this.

The journey may be long, but the destination is worth every step.

Let this chapter be a reminder that healing from DPDR, while difficult, is absolutely within your reach. With time, patience, and the right tools, you will emerge stronger and more whole than ever before. Keep moving forward, keep believing in yourself, and embrace the power that lies within you. You are on your way to a brighter future.

About the Author

Pankaj Sharma believes in the boundless magic of the universe and the extraordinary healing capabilities within each of us. Having experienced and recovered from depersonalization and derealization (DPDR) through self-discovery and understanding human psychology from deep within to heal himself, Pankaj shares his journey in this book to inspire and support others facing similar challenges. With a heartfelt commitment to guiding readers, he emphasizes the strength of the human spirit and the transformative power of resilience and self-awareness. This book is a testament to his belief that healing is not only possible but also a deeply magical journey.

Printed in Great Britain
by Amazon

727a0667-93aa-4caa-9253-2d5d2bee0f3fR01